50 British Bread Dishes for Home

By: Kelly Johnson

Table of Contents

- Scones
- Crumpets
- Tea cakes
- English muffins
- Focaccia
- Brown bread
- Wholemeal bread
- White bread
- Rustic loaf
- Soft rolls
- Bath buns
- Chelsea buns
- Lardy cake
- Cumberland sausage rolls
- Stottie cake
- Welsh cakes
- Seeded bread
- Potato bread
- Bara brith
- Lancashire hotpot bread
- Cornish pasties
- Pasty bread
- Yorkshire bread
- Eccles cakes
- Ale bread
- Derbyshire oatcakes
- Toad in the hole (with bread)
- Toasted crumpets
- Bread and butter pudding
- English trifle with sponge
- Scottish oat bread
- Cider bread
- Spicy fruit bread
- Cottage loaf
- Bloomer

- Sourdough
- Malt loaf
- Sourdough batard
- Almond bread
- Toad in the hole bread
- Apple bread
- Spelt bread
- Stollen
- Welsh rarebit (served with bread)
- Pork pie with bread
- Bread pudding
- Treacle bread
- Cinnamon and raisin bread
- Potato and rosemary bread
- Savoury scones

Scones

Ingredients:

- 2 cups (250g) all-purpose flour
- 1/4 cup (50g) granulated sugar
- 2 1/2 tsp baking powder
- 1/4 tsp salt
- 1/2 cup (115g) unsalted butter, chilled and cubed
- 1 large egg
- 1/2 cup (120ml) milk
- 1 tsp vanilla extract (optional)

Instructions:

1. Preheat oven to 425°F (220°C) and line a baking sheet with parchment paper.
2. In a bowl, mix flour, sugar, baking powder, and salt.
3. Cut in the butter until the mixture resembles coarse crumbs.
4. In a separate bowl, whisk the egg, milk, and vanilla.
5. Add wet ingredients to dry ingredients and mix gently until just combined.
6. Turn the dough out onto a floured surface, pat it into a 1-inch thick round, and cut into wedges.
7. Place the scones on the baking sheet and bake for 12-15 minutes until golden.

Crumpets

Ingredients:

- 2 cups (250g) all-purpose flour
- 1/2 tsp salt
- 1 tbsp sugar
- 2 tsp active dry yeast
- 1 1/4 cups (300ml) warm milk
- 1/4 cup (60ml) water
- 1/2 tsp baking soda

Instructions:

1. In a bowl, mix flour, salt, and sugar.
2. Dissolve yeast in warm milk and water, then add to the dry ingredients. Stir to form a thick batter.
3. Cover and let the batter rise for 1-2 hours until bubbly.
4. Heat a griddle or frying pan over medium-low heat and lightly grease with butter or oil.
5. Spoon the batter into crumpet rings and cook for 4-5 minutes until the tops are set. Flip the crumpets and cook for 1-2 more minutes.
6. Remove from the pan and serve warm with butter.

Tea Cakes

Ingredients:

- 2 1/2 cups (310g) all-purpose flour
- 1/2 tsp salt
- 2 tsp active dry yeast
- 1/4 cup (50g) sugar
- 1/4 cup (60g) unsalted butter, softened
- 1 large egg
- 3/4 cup (180ml) warm milk
- 1/2 tsp vanilla extract
- 1/2 cup (75g) currants or raisins (optional)

Instructions:

1. In a bowl, combine flour, salt, and sugar.
2. Dissolve yeast in warm milk and add to the flour mixture. Add butter, egg, and vanilla. Mix to form a dough.
3. Knead the dough for 5-7 minutes, then cover and let rise for 1 hour.
4. Punch down the dough and fold in currants or raisins, if using.
5. Roll out the dough and cut into rounds.
6. Preheat a griddle or frying pan over low heat and lightly grease it. Cook the cakes for 4-5 minutes per side until golden.
7. Serve warm with butter and jam.

English Muffins

Ingredients:

- 3 cups (375g) all-purpose flour
- 1/2 tsp salt
- 1 tbsp sugar
- 2 tsp active dry yeast
- 1 cup (240ml) warm milk
- 1/4 cup (60g) unsalted butter, melted
- 1 large egg

Instructions:

1. In a bowl, mix flour, salt, sugar, and yeast.
2. Combine warm milk, melted butter, and egg. Add the wet mixture to the dry ingredients and mix until smooth.
3. Knead the dough for 5 minutes, then cover and let rise for 1 hour.
4. Punch down the dough, roll it out to about 1/2 inch thick, and cut into rounds.
5. Heat a griddle or frying pan over medium-low heat and cook the muffins for 5-7 minutes per side until golden and cooked through.

Focaccia

Ingredients:

- 3 cups (375g) all-purpose flour
- 1 tsp salt
- 1 tbsp sugar
- 2 tsp active dry yeast
- 1 1/2 cups (360ml) warm water
- 1/4 cup (60ml) olive oil
- 2 tsp fresh rosemary (optional)

Instructions:

1. In a bowl, combine flour, salt, sugar, and yeast.
2. Add warm water and olive oil, then mix to form a dough. Knead for 5-7 minutes until smooth.
3. Cover and let the dough rise for 1-1.5 hours.
4. Preheat oven to 400°F (200°C).
5. Punch down the dough and spread it into a greased baking sheet.
6. Drizzle with olive oil and sprinkle with rosemary. Bake for 20-25 minutes until golden.

Brown Bread

Ingredients:

- 2 cups (250g) whole wheat flour
- 1 cup (125g) all-purpose flour
- 1/2 tsp salt
- 1 tbsp sugar
- 2 tsp active dry yeast
- 1 1/4 cups (300ml) warm water
- 2 tbsp olive oil

Instructions:

1. In a bowl, combine both flours, salt, and sugar.
2. Dissolve yeast in warm water and add to the dry ingredients. Mix to form a dough.
3. Knead for 5-7 minutes, then cover and let rise for 1 hour.
4. Preheat oven to 375°F (190°C).
5. Punch down the dough, shape it into a loaf, and place it in a greased loaf pan.
6. Bake for 30-35 minutes until golden and hollow when tapped.

Wholemeal Bread

Ingredients:

- 2 1/2 cups (315g) whole wheat flour
- 1 cup (125g) all-purpose flour
- 1 tsp salt
- 1 tbsp sugar
- 2 tsp active dry yeast
- 1 1/4 cups (300ml) warm water
- 2 tbsp olive oil

Instructions:

1. In a bowl, combine whole wheat flour, all-purpose flour, salt, and sugar.
2. Dissolve yeast in warm water and add to the dry ingredients. Mix to form a dough.
3. Knead for 7-10 minutes, then cover and let rise for 1 hour.
4. Preheat oven to 375°F (190°C).
5. Punch down the dough, shape it into a loaf, and place it in a greased loaf pan.
6. Bake for 30-35 minutes until golden and hollow when tapped.

White Bread

Ingredients:

- 3 cups (375g) all-purpose flour
- 1 tsp salt
- 1 tbsp sugar
- 2 tsp active dry yeast
- 1 1/4 cups (300ml) warm water
- 2 tbsp unsalted butter, softened

Instructions:

1. In a bowl, combine flour, salt, sugar, and yeast.
2. Add warm water and butter, then mix to form a dough.
3. Knead for 5-7 minutes until smooth.
4. Cover and let rise for 1-1.5 hours.
5. Preheat oven to 375°F (190°C).
6. Punch down the dough, shape it into a loaf, and place it in a greased loaf pan.
7. Bake for 25-30 minutes until golden.

Rustic Loaf

Ingredients:

- 3 cups (375g) all-purpose flour
- 1 1/2 tsp salt
- 1 tsp sugar
- 2 tsp active dry yeast
- 1 1/4 cups (300ml) warm water
- 2 tbsp olive oil

Instructions:

1. In a bowl, combine flour, salt, and sugar.
2. Dissolve yeast in warm water and add to the dry ingredients. Mix to form a dough.
3. Knead for 7-10 minutes, then cover and let rise for 1-1.5 hours.
4. Preheat oven to 450°F (230°C).
5. Punch down the dough, shape it into a round loaf, and place it on a baking sheet.
6. Bake for 25-30 minutes until golden and hollow when tapped.

Soft Rolls

Ingredients:

- 2 cups (250g) all-purpose flour
- 1 tsp salt
- 2 tsp sugar
- 1 packet (7g) active dry yeast
- 3/4 cup (180ml) warm water
- 1/4 cup (60g) unsalted butter, melted

Instructions:

1. In a bowl, combine flour, salt, and sugar.
2. Dissolve yeast in warm water and add to the dry ingredients. Mix to form a dough.
3. Knead for 5-7 minutes, then cover and let rise for 1 hour.
4. Preheat oven to 350°F (175°C).
5. Punch down the dough and shape into small rolls. Place them on a greased baking sheet.
6. Bake for 12-15 minutes until golden.

Bath Buns

Ingredients:

- 2 cups (250g) all-purpose flour
- 1/2 tsp salt
- 1/4 cup (50g) sugar
- 2 tsp active dry yeast
- 1/2 cup (120ml) warm milk
- 1/4 cup (60g) unsalted butter, softened
- 1 large egg
- 1/4 cup (40g) currants or raisins

Instructions:

1. Dissolve yeast and sugar in warm milk and let sit for 5 minutes.
2. In a bowl, combine flour, salt, butter, and egg. Add yeast mixture and knead into a dough.
3. Let the dough rise for 1 hour, then fold in currants or raisins.
4. Preheat oven to 350°F (175°C).
5. Shape dough into buns and place on a baking sheet.
6. Bake for 15-20 minutes until golden.

Chelsea Buns

Ingredients:

- 4 cups (500g) all-purpose flour
- 1/4 cup (50g) sugar
- 1 tsp salt
- 2 tsp active dry yeast
- 1 1/4 cups (300ml) warm milk
- 1/2 cup (115g) unsalted butter, softened
- 2 large eggs
- 1 cup (150g) currants or raisins
- 1 tbsp ground cinnamon
- 1/4 cup (50g) brown sugar

Instructions:

1. In a bowl, mix flour, sugar, salt, and yeast.
2. Add warm milk, butter, and eggs. Knead until smooth.
3. Let the dough rise for 1 hour, then roll it out into a rectangle.
4. Sprinkle with cinnamon, brown sugar, and currants. Roll up the dough and cut into slices.
5. Arrange the slices in a greased baking pan. Let rise for 30 minutes.
6. Preheat oven to 350°F (175°C) and bake for 25-30 minutes until golden.

Lardy Cake

Ingredients:

- 4 cups (500g) all-purpose flour
- 1/4 cup (50g) sugar
- 1 tsp salt
- 2 tsp active dry yeast
- 1 1/4 cups (300ml) warm milk
- 1/2 cup (115g) unsalted butter, softened
- 1/2 cup (115g) lard, cubed
- 2 large eggs
- 1/2 cup (75g) currants or sultanas

Instructions:

1. In a bowl, combine flour, sugar, salt, and yeast.
2. Add warm milk, butter, lard, and eggs, and knead the dough until smooth.
3. Let the dough rise for 1 hour, then roll it out into a large rectangle.
4. Sprinkle currants and fold the dough into layers.
5. Roll the dough into a loaf and place it in a greased pan. Let rise for 30 minutes.
6. Preheat oven to 350°F (175°C) and bake for 25-30 minutes until golden.

Cumberland Sausage Rolls

Ingredients:

- 1 lb (450g) Cumberland sausage meat
- 1 sheet puff pastry
- 1 egg, beaten
- 1 tbsp fresh parsley, chopped
- 1/4 tsp black pepper

Instructions:

1. Preheat oven to 375°F (190°C) and line a baking sheet with parchment paper.
2. Roll out the puff pastry and cut it into strips.
3. Season the sausage meat with parsley and black pepper, then shape it into long sausages.
4. Place the sausage onto the pastry strips and roll them up.
5. Brush the rolls with beaten egg and cut into bite-sized pieces.
6. Bake for 15-20 minutes until golden brown and cooked through.

Stottie Cake

Ingredients:

- 4 cups (500g) all-purpose flour
- 1 1/2 tsp salt
- 1 tsp sugar
- 1 packet (7g) active dry yeast
- 1 1/4 cups (300ml) warm water
- 2 tbsp olive oil

Instructions:

1. In a bowl, combine flour, salt, and sugar.
2. Dissolve yeast in warm water and add it to the flour mixture along with olive oil. Mix to form a dough.
3. Knead the dough for 5-7 minutes, then cover and let rise for 1 hour.
4. Punch down the dough and shape it into a round loaf.
5. Preheat oven to 425°F (220°C) and bake for 25-30 minutes until golden.

Welsh Cakes

Ingredients:

- 2 cups (250g) all-purpose flour
- 1/4 cup (50g) sugar
- 1 tsp baking powder
- 1/4 tsp salt
- 1/2 tsp ground cinnamon
- 1/2 cup (115g) unsalted butter, chilled and cubed
- 1 large egg
- 1/4 cup (60ml) milk
- 1/2 cup (75g) currants or sultanas

Instructions:

1. In a bowl, combine flour, sugar, baking powder, salt, and cinnamon.
2. Cut in the butter until the mixture resembles breadcrumbs.
3. Add the egg, milk, and currants. Mix to form a dough.
4. Roll out the dough on a floured surface to about 1/2-inch thickness.
5. Use a round cutter to cut into circles and cook in a lightly greased frying pan over medium heat for 2-3 minutes on each side until golden.

Seeded Bread

Ingredients:

- 3 cups (375g) all-purpose flour
- 1 tsp salt
- 1 tbsp sugar
- 2 tsp active dry yeast
- 1 1/4 cups (300ml) warm water
- 2 tbsp olive oil
- 1/4 cup (40g) mixed seeds (e.g., sunflower, pumpkin, sesame)

Instructions:

1. In a bowl, combine flour, salt, sugar, and yeast.
2. Add warm water and olive oil, then knead until smooth.
3. Let the dough rise for 1 hour.
4. Preheat oven to 375°F (190°C) and place a baking sheet inside to heat up.
5. Punch down the dough, shape it into a loaf, and sprinkle the mixed seeds on top.
6. Bake for 25-30 minutes until golden and hollow when tapped.

Potato Bread

Ingredients:

- 2 cups (250g) all-purpose flour
- 1 cup (200g) mashed potatoes
- 1 tbsp sugar
- 1 tsp salt
- 2 tsp active dry yeast
- 1/2 cup (120ml) warm water
- 1/4 cup (60g) unsalted butter, softened

Instructions:

1. In a bowl, combine flour, mashed potatoes, sugar, salt, and yeast.
2. Add warm water and butter, then mix to form a dough.
3. Knead for 5-7 minutes, then let rise for 1 hour.
4. Preheat oven to 375°F (190°C).
5. Punch down the dough, shape it into a loaf, and bake for 30-35 minutes until golden.

Bara Brith

Ingredients:

- 2 cups (250g) all-purpose flour
- 1/2 tsp baking powder
- 1/4 tsp salt
- 1 tsp mixed spice
- 1/2 cup (75g) brown sugar
- 1 1/2 cups (225g) mixed dried fruit (raisins, sultanas, currants)
- 1/2 cup (120ml) warm tea
- 1 large egg
- 1 tbsp unsalted butter, melted

Instructions:

1. Preheat oven to 350°F (175°C) and grease a loaf pan.
2. In a bowl, combine flour, baking powder, salt, mixed spice, and sugar.
3. Stir in the dried fruit.
4. In a separate bowl, mix tea, egg, and melted butter.
5. Combine the wet ingredients with the dry ingredients and mix until well combined.
6. Pour the batter into the pan and bake for 35-40 minutes until golden.

Lancashire Hotpot Bread

Ingredients:

- 3 cups (375g) all-purpose flour
- 1 tsp salt
- 1 tbsp sugar
- 1 packet (7g) active dry yeast
- 1 1/4 cups (300ml) warm water
- 2 tbsp olive oil

Instructions:

1. In a bowl, combine flour, salt, sugar, and yeast.
2. Add warm water and olive oil, then knead until smooth.
3. Let the dough rise for 1 hour.
4. Preheat oven to 375°F (190°C) and shape the dough into a round loaf.
5. Place the loaf on a greased baking sheet and bake for 25-30 minutes.

Cornish Pasties

Ingredients:

For the dough:

- 2 1/2 cups (310g) all-purpose flour
- 1/2 tsp salt
- 1/2 cup (115g) unsalted butter, chilled and cubed
- 1/4 cup (60ml) cold water

For the filling:

- 1/2 lb (225g) ground beef
- 1 medium potato, diced
- 1 small onion, chopped
- 1/4 cup (60ml) beef broth
- Salt and pepper to taste

Instructions:

1. Preheat oven to 375°F (190°C) and line a baking sheet with parchment paper.
2. For the dough: Mix flour and salt, then cut in the butter until crumbly. Add cold water and mix until dough forms.
3. For the filling: Mix ground beef, diced potatoes, onion, beef broth, salt, and pepper.
4. Roll out the dough and cut into rounds. Place filling in the center and fold the dough over to seal.
5. Bake for 25-30 minutes until golden.

Pasty Bread

Ingredients:

- 3 cups (375g) all-purpose flour
- 1 tsp salt
- 1 tbsp sugar
- 2 tsp active dry yeast
- 1 1/4 cups (300ml) warm water
- 1/4 cup (60g) unsalted butter, softened

Instructions:

1. In a bowl, combine flour, salt, sugar, and yeast.
2. Add warm water and butter, then knead into a smooth dough.
3. Let the dough rise for 1 hour.
4. Preheat oven to 375°F (190°C).
5. Punch down the dough, shape it into a loaf, and bake for 25-30 minutes until golden.

Yorkshire Bread

Ingredients:

- 2 cups (250g) all-purpose flour
- 1 tsp salt
- 1 tbsp sugar
- 1 packet (7g) active dry yeast
- 1 1/4 cups (300ml) warm water
- 2 tbsp unsalted butter, softened

Instructions:

1. In a bowl, combine flour, salt, sugar, and yeast.
2. Add warm water and butter, knead into a smooth dough.
3. Let the dough rise for 1 hour.
4. Preheat oven to 375°F (190°C).
5. Punch down the dough, shape it into a round loaf, and bake for 25-30 minutes until golden.

Eccles Cakes

Ingredients:

- 2 cups (250g) all-purpose flour
- 1/2 tsp salt
- 1/2 cup (115g) unsalted butter, chilled and cubed
- 1/4 cup (60g) granulated sugar
- 1/4 cup (60ml) cold water
- 1 cup (150g) currants
- 2 tbsp brown sugar
- 1/4 tsp ground nutmeg
- 1/2 tsp ground cinnamon
- 1 tbsp milk (for brushing)

Instructions:

1. Preheat oven to 375°F (190°C) and line a baking sheet with parchment paper.
2. For the dough: Mix flour and salt. Cut in the butter until crumbly, then add sugar. Gradually add water and mix to form a dough.
3. Roll the dough out into a thin rectangle.
4. For the filling: Mix currants, brown sugar, cinnamon, and nutmeg. Place the filling in the center of the dough and fold the edges over.
5. Cut into rounds, place them on the baking sheet, and brush with milk.
6. Bake for 15-18 minutes until golden.

Ale Bread

Ingredients:

- 3 cups (375g) all-purpose flour
- 1 tsp salt
- 1 tbsp sugar
- 1 packet (7g) active dry yeast
- 1 1/2 cups (360ml) ale (room temperature)
- 2 tbsp unsalted butter, melted

Instructions:

1. Preheat oven to 375°F (190°C) and grease a loaf pan.
2. In a bowl, combine flour, salt, and sugar.
3. Dissolve yeast in ale and add to the dry ingredients, followed by melted butter. Mix until dough forms.
4. Knead the dough for 5-7 minutes, then let rise for 1 hour.
5. Punch down the dough, shape it into a loaf, and place it in the pan.
6. Bake for 30-35 minutes, or until golden and hollow when tapped.

Derbyshire Oatcakes

Ingredients:

- 2 cups (250g) rolled oats
- 1 cup (125g) all-purpose flour
- 1/2 tsp salt
- 1 tsp baking powder
- 1/2 cup (120ml) milk
- 1/2 cup (115g) unsalted butter, melted
- 1/2 cup (60g) sugar

Instructions:

1. Preheat oven to 375°F (190°C) and grease a baking sheet.
2. In a bowl, combine oats, flour, salt, and baking powder.
3. Add milk, melted butter, and sugar, then mix until a dough forms.
4. Roll out the dough on a floured surface and cut into rounds.
5. Place the oatcakes on the baking sheet and bake for 10-12 minutes until golden.

Toad in the Hole (with Bread)

Ingredients:

- 6 sausages
- 1 cup (125g) all-purpose flour
- 1/2 tsp salt
- 1/2 tsp ground black pepper
- 1 tsp baking powder
- 2 eggs
- 1 cup (240ml) milk
- 2 tbsp vegetable oil

Instructions:

1. Preheat oven to 400°F (200°C) and heat the oil in a baking dish.
2. Brown sausages in a pan over medium heat, then place them in the baking dish.
3. In a bowl, whisk flour, salt, pepper, baking powder, eggs, and milk into a batter.
4. Pour the batter over the sausages and bake for 25-30 minutes until puffed and golden.

Toasted Crumpets

Ingredients:

- 1 batch crumpet dough (as described earlier)

Instructions:

1. Prepare crumpets according to your preferred recipe.
2. Once cooked, place them under a broiler or on a hot griddle until golden and toasted.
3. Serve warm with butter and jam.

Bread and Butter Pudding

Ingredients:

- 6 slices of stale white bread
- 1/2 cup (100g) unsalted butter, softened
- 1/2 cup (100g) sugar
- 2 1/2 cups (600ml) milk
- 3 large eggs
- 1 tsp vanilla extract
- 1/4 tsp ground cinnamon (optional)
- 1/4 cup (50g) raisins or currants

Instructions:

1. Preheat oven to 350°F (175°C) and grease a baking dish.
2. Butter the bread slices and arrange them in the baking dish.
3. In a bowl, whisk together milk, eggs, sugar, vanilla extract, and cinnamon.
4. Pour the egg mixture over the bread and let it soak for 10-15 minutes.
5. Sprinkle raisins on top, then bake for 30-35 minutes until golden.

English Trifle with Sponge

Ingredients:

For the sponge cake:

- 1 cup (125g) all-purpose flour
- 1/2 cup (100g) granulated sugar
- 3 large eggs
- 1 tsp vanilla extract

For the trifle layers:

- 1 1/2 cups (360ml) custard (store-bought or homemade)
- 1 cup (240ml) heavy cream, whipped
- 1/2 cup (120ml) fruit (e.g., berries, peaches)
- 1/2 cup (120ml) fruit jelly (optional)

Instructions:

1. Preheat oven to 350°F (175°C) and grease a baking pan.
2. For the sponge cake: Beat eggs and sugar until thick and pale. Add vanilla extract and gradually fold in the flour.
3. Bake for 20-25 minutes, then allow the cake to cool.
4. Cut the sponge into cubes and layer in a trifle dish.
5. Layer with custard, whipped cream, fruit, and optional fruit jelly. Repeat the layers.
6. Chill for 2-3 hours before serving.

Scottish Oat Bread

Ingredients:

- 2 cups (250g) rolled oats
- 2 cups (250g) whole wheat flour
- 1 1/2 tsp salt
- 1 tsp baking powder
- 1/4 cup (60ml) warm water
- 1/4 cup (60ml) milk
- 2 tbsp unsalted butter, melted

Instructions:

1. Preheat oven to 375°F (190°C) and grease a loaf pan.
2. In a bowl, combine oats, whole wheat flour, salt, and baking powder.
3. Add warm water, milk, and melted butter, mixing to form a dough.
4. Knead the dough for 5-7 minutes, then shape it into a loaf.
5. Bake for 30-35 minutes until golden and hollow when tapped.

Cider Bread

Ingredients:

- 3 cups (375g) all-purpose flour
- 1 tsp salt
- 1 tbsp sugar
- 2 tsp active dry yeast
- 1 cup (240ml) cider
- 2 tbsp unsalted butter, melted

Instructions:

1. In a bowl, combine flour, salt, sugar, and yeast.
2. Add cider and melted butter, mixing to form a dough.
3. Knead the dough for 5-7 minutes, then cover and let rise for 1 hour.
4. Preheat oven to 375°F (190°C).
5. Punch down the dough, shape it into a loaf, and bake for 25-30 minutes until golden.

Spicy Fruit Bread

Ingredients:

- 2 cups (250g) all-purpose flour
- 1 tsp ground cinnamon
- 1/2 tsp ground nutmeg
- 1/2 tsp ground allspice
- 1/2 tsp salt
- 1/4 cup (50g) brown sugar
- 1 1/2 cups (225g) mixed dried fruit (raisins, currants, dried apricots)
- 1/2 cup (120ml) warm water
- 1 packet (7g) active dry yeast
- 2 tbsp unsalted butter, melted

Instructions:

1. Preheat oven to 350°F (175°C) and grease a loaf pan.
2. In a bowl, combine flour, cinnamon, nutmeg, allspice, salt, and sugar.
3. Dissolve yeast in warm water and add to the dry ingredients along with melted butter. Mix to form a dough.
4. Knead for 5-7 minutes, then let rise for 1 hour.
5. Punch down the dough, fold in dried fruit, shape it into a loaf, and bake for 30-35 minutes until golden.

Cottage Loaf

Ingredients:

- 4 cups (500g) all-purpose flour
- 1 tsp salt
- 2 tsp active dry yeast
- 1/4 cup (50g) granulated sugar
- 1 1/4 cups (300ml) warm water
- 2 tbsp unsalted butter, melted

Instructions:

1. In a bowl, combine flour, salt, yeast, and sugar.
2. Add warm water and melted butter, then knead until smooth.
3. Let the dough rise for 1 hour, then punch it down.
4. Shape the dough into two balls and place one on top of the other.
5. Preheat oven to 375°F (190°C) and bake for 25-30 minutes until golden.

Bloomer

Ingredients:

- 4 cups (500g) all-purpose flour
- 1 1/2 tsp salt
- 2 tsp active dry yeast
- 1 tbsp sugar
- 1 1/4 cups (300ml) warm water
- 2 tbsp unsalted butter, softened

Instructions:

1. Preheat oven to 375°F (190°C) and grease a loaf pan.
2. In a bowl, combine flour, salt, sugar, and yeast.
3. Add warm water and butter, then knead until smooth.
4. Let the dough rise for 1 hour.
5. Punch down the dough, shape it into a loaf, and place it in the pan.
6. Let the dough rise for another 30 minutes, then bake for 30-35 minutes until golden.

Sourdough

Ingredients:

- 1 cup (240g) sourdough starter (see below)
- 3 cups (375g) all-purpose flour
- 1 tsp salt
- 1 1/2 cups (360ml) warm water

Sourdough Starter (makes 1 cup):

- 1/2 cup (60g) whole wheat flour
- 1/2 cup (120ml) water
- 1 tbsp active dry yeast

Instructions:

1. To make the starter: In a bowl, combine whole wheat flour and water. Stir until smooth. Cover and let sit for 24 hours at room temperature.
2. Add yeast to the mixture and stir again. Cover and let sit for another 24 hours, stirring daily.
3. For the dough: In a bowl, combine sourdough starter, flour, salt, and warm water. Mix until smooth and knead for 10 minutes.
4. Let the dough rise for 1-2 hours.
5. Shape the dough into a loaf and place it in a greased pan. Let rise for another hour.
6. Preheat oven to 375°F (190°C) and bake for 30-35 minutes until golden.

Malt Loaf

Ingredients:

- 2 cups (250g) all-purpose flour
- 1 tsp baking powder
- 1/4 tsp salt
- 1/2 cup (100g) malt extract
- 1/2 cup (120ml) warm water
- 1/2 cup (75g) dried fruit (raisins, currants)
- 1/4 cup (50g) brown sugar
- 1 egg

Instructions:

1. Preheat oven to 350°F (175°C) and grease a loaf pan.
2. In a bowl, combine flour, baking powder, and salt.
3. In a separate bowl, whisk together malt extract, warm water, sugar, and egg.
4. Add the wet ingredients to the dry ingredients and mix until smooth.
5. Fold in dried fruit.
6. Pour the batter into the loaf pan and bake for 45-50 minutes until golden.

Sourdough Bâtard

Ingredients:

- 2 cups (240g) sourdough starter
- 3 cups (375g) all-purpose flour
- 1 tsp salt
- 1 cup (240ml) warm water

Instructions:

1. In a bowl, combine sourdough starter, flour, salt, and warm water. Knead until smooth.
2. Let the dough rise for 4-6 hours at room temperature, or overnight in the refrigerator.
3. Punch down the dough and shape it into a bâtard (a long, oval loaf).
4. Place the dough on a greased baking sheet and let it rise for another 1-2 hours.
5. Preheat oven to 375°F (190°C) and bake for 25-30 minutes until golden and hollow when tapped.

Almond Bread

Ingredients:

- 2 cups (250g) all-purpose flour
- 1/2 cup (100g) almond meal
- 1/2 tsp salt
- 1 tsp baking powder
- 1/2 cup (115g) unsalted butter, softened
- 1 cup (200g) granulated sugar
- 3 large eggs
- 1 tsp vanilla extract
- 1/2 cup (120ml) milk

Instructions:

1. Preheat oven to 350°F (175°C) and grease a loaf pan.
2. In a bowl, mix flour, almond meal, salt, and baking powder.
3. In another bowl, beat butter and sugar until smooth. Add eggs one at a time, followed by vanilla extract.
4. Gradually add the dry ingredients and mix until combined. Add milk and mix until smooth.
5. Pour the batter into the loaf pan and bake for 45-50 minutes until golden.

Toad in the Hole Bread

Ingredients:

For the bread batter:

- 2 cups (250g) all-purpose flour
- 1 tsp salt
- 1 tsp baking powder
- 1 cup (240ml) milk
- 1 egg

For the sausages:

- 6 sausages (preferably British sausages)
- 2 tbsp vegetable oil

Instructions:

1. Preheat oven to 400°F (200°C).
2. Heat oil in a pan over medium heat and cook the sausages until browned.
3. In a bowl, mix flour, salt, baking powder, milk, and egg to form a batter.
4. Place sausages in a baking dish and pour the batter over the sausages.
5. Bake for 30-35 minutes until the batter is puffed and golden.

Apple Bread

Ingredients:

- 2 cups (250g) all-purpose flour
- 1 tsp baking powder
- 1/2 tsp cinnamon
- 1/4 tsp salt
- 1 cup (200g) granulated sugar
- 1/2 cup (120ml) milk
- 1/2 cup (115g) unsalted butter, softened
- 2 large eggs
- 1 cup (150g) diced apples

Instructions:

1. Preheat oven to 350°F (175°C) and grease a loaf pan.
2. In a bowl, combine flour, baking powder, cinnamon, and salt.
3. In another bowl, beat butter and sugar until smooth. Add eggs one at a time, then add milk.
4. Gradually add the dry ingredients and mix until smooth. Fold in diced apples.
5. Pour the batter into the loaf pan and bake for 45-50 minutes until golden.

Spelt Bread

Ingredients:

- 2 cups (250g) spelt flour
- 1 1/2 cups (190g) all-purpose flour
- 1 tsp salt
- 1 tbsp sugar
- 2 tsp active dry yeast
- 1 1/4 cups (300ml) warm water
- 2 tbsp olive oil

Instructions:

1. In a bowl, combine spelt flour, all-purpose flour, salt, sugar, and yeast.
2. Add warm water and olive oil, then knead until smooth.
3. Let the dough rise for 1 hour.
4. Preheat oven to 375°F (190°C).
5. Punch down the dough, shape it into a loaf, and bake for 25-30 minutes until golden.

Stollen

Ingredients:

- 3 cups (375g) all-purpose flour
- 1/2 tsp salt
- 1/2 cup (100g) sugar
- 1 packet (7g) active dry yeast
- 1 cup (240ml) warm milk
- 1/2 cup (115g) unsalted butter, softened
- 2 large eggs
- 1 cup (150g) mixed dried fruit
- 1/2 cup (75g) chopped nuts (almonds, walnuts)
- 1/2 tsp ground cinnamon
- 1/4 tsp ground nutmeg

Instructions:

1. Preheat oven to 350°F (175°C) and grease a baking sheet.
2. In a bowl, mix flour, salt, sugar, yeast, cinnamon, and nutmeg.
3. Add warm milk, butter, and eggs, then knead the dough until smooth.
4. Add dried fruit and nuts, then let the dough rise for 1 hour.
5. Shape the dough into a loaf and bake for 30-35 minutes until golden.

Welsh Rarebit (served with Bread)

Ingredients:

- 2 tbsp unsalted butter
- 1 tbsp all-purpose flour
- 1 cup (240ml) milk
- 1 cup (120g) sharp cheddar cheese, grated
- 1 tsp Dijon mustard
- 1/2 tsp Worcestershire sauce
- 1 egg, beaten
- 4 slices of bread, toasted

Instructions:

1. In a pan, melt butter and add flour to create a roux. Cook for 1-2 minutes.
2. Gradually add milk, whisking until thickened.
3. Add cheese, mustard, and Worcestershire sauce, and stir until the cheese is melted.
4. Remove from heat and stir in the beaten egg.
5. Pour the sauce over toasted bread and serve immediately.

Pork Pie with Bread

Ingredients:

- 1 1/2 lbs (680g) ground pork
- 1/4 lb (115g) pork fat, diced
- 1 tsp salt
- 1/2 tsp ground black pepper
- 1/2 tsp thyme
- 1 sheet puff pastry
- 1 egg, beaten

Instructions:

1. Preheat oven to 375°F (190°C) and grease a pie pan.
2. In a bowl, mix ground pork, pork fat, salt, pepper, and thyme.
3. Roll out puff pastry and line the pie pan with it.
4. Fill with the pork mixture and cover with a pastry top.
5. Brush with beaten egg and bake for 45-50 minutes until golden.

Bread Pudding

Ingredients:

- 4 cups (500g) stale bread, cubed
- 2 cups (480ml) whole milk
- 1/2 cup (100g) sugar
- 3 large eggs
- 1 tsp vanilla extract
- 1/2 tsp ground cinnamon
- 1/2 cup (75g) raisins

Instructions:

1. Preheat oven to 350°F (175°C) and grease a baking dish.
2. In a bowl, whisk together milk, sugar, eggs, vanilla extract, and cinnamon.
3. Add the cubed bread and raisins, and let soak for 10 minutes.
4. Pour the mixture into the baking dish and bake for 35-40 minutes until set and golden.

Treacle Bread

Ingredients:

- 3 cups (375g) all-purpose flour
- 1 1/2 tsp baking powder
- 1/2 tsp salt
- 1 tbsp sugar
- 1/2 cup (120ml) dark treacle (molasses)
- 1/2 cup (120ml) warm milk
- 2 tbsp unsalted butter, softened
- 1 large egg

Instructions:

1. Preheat oven to 375°F (190°C) and grease a loaf pan.
2. In a bowl, combine flour, baking powder, salt, and sugar.
3. In another bowl, mix together treacle, milk, butter, and egg until smooth.
4. Gradually add the wet ingredients to the dry ingredients and mix until just combined.
5. Pour the batter into the loaf pan and bake for 30-35 minutes until golden and a toothpick comes out clean.

Cinnamon and Raisin Bread

Ingredients:

- 3 cups (375g) all-purpose flour
- 1 tsp salt
- 1 tbsp sugar
- 2 tsp active dry yeast
- 1 cup (240ml) warm milk
- 2 tbsp unsalted butter, softened
- 1/2 cup (75g) raisins
- 1 tbsp ground cinnamon
- 1 large egg

Instructions:

1. Preheat oven to 375°F (190°C) and grease a loaf pan.
2. In a bowl, combine flour, salt, sugar, yeast, and cinnamon.
3. Add warm milk, butter, and egg, then knead the dough for 5-7 minutes until smooth.
4. Gently fold in raisins.
5. Let the dough rise for 1 hour.
6. Punch down the dough, shape it into a loaf, and place it in the pan. Let rise for another 30 minutes.
7. Bake for 25-30 minutes until golden and hollow when tapped.

Potato and Rosemary Bread

Ingredients:

- 2 cups (250g) all-purpose flour
- 1 cup (150g) mashed potatoes (cooled)
- 1 tbsp fresh rosemary, chopped
- 1 tsp salt
- 1 tbsp sugar
- 1 tsp active dry yeast
- 1/2 cup (120ml) warm water
- 2 tbsp olive oil

Instructions:

1. Preheat oven to 375°F (190°C) and grease a baking sheet.
2. In a bowl, combine flour, mashed potatoes, rosemary, salt, and sugar.
3. Dissolve yeast in warm water and add to the dry ingredients along with olive oil. Mix to form a dough.
4. Knead for 7-10 minutes until smooth.
5. Let the dough rise for 1 hour.
6. Shape the dough into a loaf and place it on the prepared baking sheet. Let rise for another 30 minutes.
7. Bake for 25-30 minutes until golden.

Savoury Scones

Ingredients:

- 2 cups (250g) all-purpose flour
- 1 tbsp baking powder
- 1/2 tsp salt
- 1/4 tsp ground black pepper
- 1/2 cup (120g) unsalted butter, chilled and cubed
- 1 cup (100g) grated cheddar cheese
- 1/2 cup (120ml) milk
- 1 large egg
- 1 tbsp fresh chives, chopped (optional)

Instructions:

1. Preheat oven to 425°F (220°C) and line a baking sheet with parchment paper.
2. In a bowl, combine flour, baking powder, salt, and pepper.
3. Cut in the butter until the mixture resembles coarse crumbs.
4. Stir in cheese and chives, if using.
5. Add milk and egg, mixing gently until just combined.
6. Turn the dough out onto a floured surface, pat it into a 1-inch thick round, and cut into wedges.
7. Place the scones on the baking sheet and bake for 12-15 minutes until golden.

www.ingramcontent.com/pod-product-compliance
Lightning Source LLC
LaVergne TN
LVHW081332060526
838201LV00055B/2598